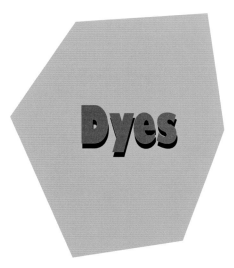
Dyes

DYES

FROM SEA SNAILS
TO SYNTHETICS

RUTH G. KASSINGER

Material World

Twenty-First Century Books
Brookfield, Connecticut

To my parents,
Alice and Henry Good

Cover photograph courtesy of © Sergio Spada/Graphistock
Photographs courtesy of © George Payne www.cajunimages.com: p. 4; Photo Researchers, Inc.: pp. 6 (© François Ducasse/Rapho), 13 (© Jean-Loup Charmet/SPL), 30 (© John Watney), 40 (© Scott Camazine), 53 (© David T. Roberts); SuperStock: pp. 8 (Holton Collection), 10 (top © Lissette Le Bon; bottom © Steve Vidler), 22, 45 (© Nora Scarlett), 46 (PeterWilli/Musée du Louvre, Paris), 69, 71 (bottom © Charles Orrico); The Bridgeman Art Library: pp. 9, 55, 65 (Russell-Cotes Art Gallery and Museum, Bournemouth, UK) ; Photri-Microstock: pp. 11 (© Vic Bider), 68; PhotoEdit: pp. 18 (© Bonnie Kamin), 70 (© Jeff Greenberg), 71 (left © David Young-Wolff; right © Tom McCarthy); Alinari/Art Resource, NY: p. 20; Werner Forman/Art Resource, NY: p. 24 (© Nick Saunders); Visuals Unlimited, Inc.: p. 29 (© Robert E. Lyons); © Paul Monfile: p. 32; A. M. Rosati/Art Resource, NY: p. 35; Tom Pantages: pp. 38, 41, 42; Getty Images: p. 48 (Hulton/Archive); Scala/Art Resource, NY: pp. 51, 59. Map by Joe LeMonnier.

Library of Congress Cataloging-in-Publication Data
Kassinger, Ruth, 1954-
Dyes : from sea snails to synthetics / Ruth G. Kassinger.
p. cm. — (Material world)
Summary: Explains how dyes were developed, how they have been used throughout history and discusses the history and folklore surrounding different colors.
Includes bibliographical references and index.
ISBN 0-7613-2112-8 (library binding)
1. Dyes and dyeing—Juvenile literature. [1. Dyes and dyeing—History. 2. Color.] I. Title.
TT854.3 .K37 2003   667'.2—dc21   2002002102

Published by Twenty-First Century Books
A Division of The Millbrook Press, Inc.
2 Old New Milford Road
Brookfield, Connecticut 06804
www.millbrookpress.com

Modern calico fabric

Contents

Stone Age people used red ocher to create these animal images on cave walls in France.

CHAPTER ONE

The Meaning of Color

SPEAKING WITH COLOR

About 24,500 years ago in what is today Portugal, a four-year-old boy died and was buried. The boy's family dug a shallow grave with sticks and stone tools and placed the boy's body in it. Then they covered his body with powdered red ocher, a red mineral dug from the earth. They added a pierced shell and then filled in the grave site with dirt.

Why did they sprinkle red ocher on the body? These people would have known that when too much red blood escapes the bodies of living creatures, they die. They would have known that the presence of red blood in the body means life. We'll never know for sure why the family of the boy took care to bury him in red ocher, but we can guess. The red mineral was probably a symbol for blood, and was meant to provide for life after death for their child.

Archaeologists (scientists who study past cultures by examining their tools, pottery, and other remains) have found red ocher powder on the floors of caves and at ancient campsites from Australia to Europe to the Americas. We know that the people who gathered the ocher mixed it—as well as charcoal, chalk, and clay—with animal fat to make paint they used on cave walls. We can guess, from our knowledge of primitive tribes' customs, that prehistoric people also used some of this red ocher to paint their bodies.

To prepare for a dance mourning death, this New Guinea girl painted her face in red, white, and black stripes.

Today, people in some tribal communities color their skin with paints, both as ways to recognize one another and to separate themselves from outsiders. They also paint themselves, as their ancestors have done, with particular colors to celebrate rituals and highlight important events. For example, in ceremonies celebrating adolescence, girls in New Guinea are painted in red-and-white stripes. Some Australian aboriginal tribes paint adolescent girls in blotches of red, yellow, and white. Adolescent boys of the Xhosa tribe in southern Africa are painted all white.

Among some tribal groups, warriors often painted themselves in colored patterns to appear frighteningly inhuman or supernatural to their enemies. In ancient Britain, the Picts scared the Romans by painting themselves blue. In Africa, the Masai painted half their bodies red and the other half white, and the Wagogo circled one eye in red and the other in black. Native American tribes used blue, black, red, and white face paints made from plant roots, clay, and buffalo fat. All over the globe and for thousands of years, people have painted their bodies in different colors to send a message to people looking at them.

In his painting Pictish Man Holding a Human Head, *the sixteenth-century artist John White shows how the Picts painted themselves to look fierce.*

9

People today still use color to identify themselves as members of a group. These sports fans wear the colors of their team. Soldiers in specially trained units of the U.S. Army wear colored berets to signal their membership in these elite groups. Airborne units wear maroon berets, Special Forces wear green, and Rangers wear tan. Around the world, Buddhist monks wear saffron-colored (yellow-orange) robes. The Scots wear tartan plaid kilts whose colors identify the wearer's ties to a particular clan (family group).

Painted sports fans

Buddhist monks
in traditional robes

COLOR, MYTH, AND MAGIC

In many early religions, gods and spirits became associated with certain colors. Often, because sunshine and good harvests went together, gods of the sun and harvests were pictured wearing yellow and gold. Ceres, the Roman goddess of agriculture, was frequently pictured in yellow or gold robes. Blood, war, and red went together, and in Roman mythology, the reddish planet Mars and the god of war Mars were linked. In many mythologies the cool, white moon represented purity, and people pictured the gods who

In many cultures white is the color of bridal gowns.

protected young girls and virginity wearing white. White is still the color of bridal gowns in many European and North American cultures.

Once people associated particular gods and spirits with certain colors, it took only a small leap of imagination to believe that colors themselves had magical powers. Before modern medicine, no one knew what caused disease, and many people believed evil spirits caused illness. It made sense, therefore, to try to treat disease with magic, and often the treatment involved color.

Many people believed that a disease involving a color could be cured by applying the same color. In Germany, jaundice (a liver disease that makes the skin yellowish) was treated with yellow turnips. In England, yellow spiders rolled in butter treated the same disease. In the Arab world, yellow flowers were supposed to cure diseases of the urinary system, and red flowers were used to treat diseases of the blood.

Red was the color of choice in treating illness, and red-dyed cloth was frequently prescribed. The famous eleventh-century Persian philosopher and physician Avicenna dressed his patients in red. In Ireland and Russia, doctors treated scarlet fever patients by covering them in red flannel. On the Greek island of Kárpathos, illness was treated by tying a red thread around a sick person's neck. (Friends later untied the string and retied it to a tree to transfer the illness to the tree.) In Macedonia, red yarn was attached to the bedroom door of a mother and newborn to ward off evil spirits. Red was so popular a cure that until the nineteenth century, English physicians wore scarlet cloaks as a mark of their profession.

White was a practical color for Egyptian linen. Linen is a tough fiber, and so it stood up to cleaning by boiling in water. Boiling would have removed dyes from linen since most dyes don't bond well with the tough flax fibers. Although the Egyptians could have redyed their clothing from time to time, it was convenient that white was the fashionable color!

The Egyptians were early experts in weaving fibers of the flax plant into linen cloth. For thousands of years, Egyptian men and women, from slaves to the pharaoh, wore pleated white linen skirts or robes. We know they knew how to dye linen because red- and yellow-dyed linen has been found in the earliest pharaohs' tombs, but the Egyptians purposefully wore white for most occasions. Egyptian linen is naturally gray, so it had to be

In this seventeenth-century engraving, a physician dressed in a red robe, the mark of his profession, tapes a woman's arm prior to bloodletting, a procedure used to treat various ailments.

bleached with natron or potash (two naturally occurring chemicals) to make it white. White linen became a symbol of the divine purity of Isis, the goddess of creation, life, and flax.

COLOR AND RANK

For thousands of years, a deep purplish red was the color of royalty in the Middle East and Europe. This color was called *blatta,* or "color of congealed blood," by the ancient Greeks. It was first made in quantity from the mucus of the *Murex branclaris, Murex trunculus,* and *Purpura haemastoma* sea snails by the ancient Phoenicians about 1200 B.C. Because thousands of sea snails were needed to make small amounts of the dye, the color was very expensive. Only people of great wealth could afford clothes dyed in what became known as "Tyrian purple" (named after the Phoenician city of Tyre).

The ancient Greeks thought purple was the noblest color, and generals and statesmen wore robes colored with the sea snail dye. Tyrian purple was the color of wealth and power when Rome rose to become an international power after 300 B.C. High Roman officials wore the *clavi,* or purple stripes, to demonstrate their importance. In 46 B.C., the first Roman emperor, Julius Caesar, restricted the wearing of purple in ancient Rome. Only members of the immediate ruling circle could wear purple. In about A.D. 60, Emperor Nero made its manufacture an imperial monopoly and forbade anyone outside the royal family—on pain of death—to wear it.

Even after the fall of the Roman Empire in about A.D. 500, purple remained the color of royalty. The Byzantine emperors made purple the color of their authority, too, and monopolized its production. A child of a Byzantine emperor was said to have been "to the purple born." Purple also became the color of the high-ranking Christian clergy. The pope and cardinals wore purple.

Bright red is another color that has denoted wealth and rank since ancient times. The bright red dye made from the *kermes* (pronounced *KUR-meez*) insect that lived on scrubby oak trees around the Mediterranean Sea and in Asia Minor was also very expensive. In ancient Rome, it would have taken a stonemason about a month to earn enough money to buy enough bright red wool to make a tunic. After Constantinople, the capital of the Byzantine Empire, was captured by the Turks in 1453, the secret of dyeing purple with sea snails was lost. So bright red then became the favored color of royalty and nobility. In 1464 the pope decreed that cardinals would wear "cardinal's purple" robes, which were actually bright red dyed with kermes!

From the fifteenth through the seventeenth centuries, people outside the nobility began to accumulate wealth. Merchants, traders, and professionals not born to the upper class gained

According to an ancient Phoenician legend, the god Melqart longed for the love of a beautiful sea nymph named Tyrus. Tyrus liked Melqart, but it seems she was content with friendship. One day, Melqart and Tyrus were walking by the shores of the Mediterranean Sea when they saw Melqart's dog toying with a large spiky seashell. Melqart called to his dog, who dropped the seashell and came running back to him. When the dog arrived, Tyrus saw that its muzzle was stained a beautiful shade of purple. Tyrus had never seen such a color, and she quickly offered Melqart a bargain. If he would bring her a robe dyed in the same beautiful color, she would marry him. Melqart immediately agreed. He collected more of the sea snails, extracted the dye, and, so the legend goes, started the famous Phoenician purple dye industry.

enough riches to buy clothes in the rich colors that previously only the nobility had been able to afford. It was no longer clear at a glance who was born of noble blood and who was not. Members of royal and noble families were not pleased with that, and rulers throughout Europe created *sumptuary laws* to deal with the problem. Sumptuary laws regulated who could purchase or own certain goods. Many of these laws dealt with clothes and concerned the specific fabrics, styles, and colors that could or could not be worn. In England in the 1500s, for example, no one except dukes, marquesses, earls, barons, and knights could wear velvet silk or any clothes in crimson, scarlet, or blue. Only countesses and women of higher rank could wear purple silk. In France, a law of 1328 allowed princes and knights to wear scarlet, but then in the fifteenth century scarlet became a color strictly for the king. In fifteenth-century Scotland, working-people were limited to gray and white on working days, but could wear light blue, green, and red on holidays.

People in Asia were just as sensitive as Europeans to the messages conveyed by color. In Japan, the crown prince Shotoku changed the course of Japanese history in A.D. 604 when he established the "Twelve-Cap Ranking System." Before Shotoku, a person's rank at the Japanese royal court was inherited. Shotoku established a new system that was based on an individual's merit and loyalty to the emperor. The twelve possible ranks, each of which had specific privileges at court, were identified by caps colored in light and dark shades of purple, green, red, yellow, white, and black.

Color in the broader ancient Japanese society also held great meaning. In the Heian era (794–1185), the distinctions became even more sophisticated and complicated. Women might wear as many as twelve differently colored silk robes at a time. The sleeves were of different lengths so that a strip of each one would be visible. Each subtle shade of color had to be exactly right, according to the woman's social position, or scandal might result.

The Chinese emperors of the Qing dynasty (1644–1911) had a keen sense of the political and social importance of color. Only the emperor could wear yellow (the color of the sun), and only the crown prince wore orange (the reflected glow of the sun). Lesser members of the royal house wore lustrous silk dyed in other strong colors, such as bright blue, red, and purple. These bright colors were forbidden to merchants, even if they had the money to buy dyed silk, and to the common people, most of whom could only afford to wear gray and beige clothes anyway. In China during the Qing dynasty, you could tell a person's place in society just by the color of his or her clothes.

HAIR DYES

Humans have colored their hair for a long time. Some Egyptians used a plant-based dye called *henna* to redden their hair. Other ancient hair coloring formulas included sage, indigo, and chamomile. During the Renaissance, upper-class women colored their hair blond because angels were always portrayed as blonds. They spread a mixture of black sulfur, alum, and honey on their hair and let the sun fall on their tresses. Once chlorine was discovered and chlorine bleaches were invented in the late 1700s, women lightened their hair with bleach. Men have not been immune from the urge to color

A modern
fashion statement—
dyed red hair

their hair for cosmetic purposes. In the 1800s men used silver-nitrate-based formulas to darken their mustaches and hair.

The French chemist Eugene Schuller developed a new kind of hair coloring in 1909 based on paraphenylenediamine, a new chemical. He founded a company that became known as L'Oreal, which is still a major hair products company. There are two chemicals that are present in all permanent color formulas: hydrogen peroxide, which bleaches the hair, and ammonia. When the ammonia and peroxide react with each other, a new color is created and deposited in the individual hairs.

Today, people experiment with many non-permanent colors in a range of wild colors. These colors are not truly dyes because they do not penetrate the hairs, but instead coat their exteriors. They will wash off after a number of shampooings.

FLAGS

Some time during the first millennium, the Chinese and Indians developed the idea of flags. At first, flags represented rulers. As a consequence, flags were given the respect due to the ruler. In ancient China, it was a crime to touch the flag, just as it was a crime to touch the ruler. On the ancient battlefields of India, capturing the enemy's flag was an important military objective. When an army's flag disappeared, the troops became confused and demoralized. The loss of an army's flag often meant impending defeat.

Vexillologists (people who study flags) believe that flags evolved from wooden staffs (poles) that were carved and decorated with symbols of a tribe or group. The tribal leader carried the tribe's staff, which was decorated with carvings, feathers, and braided strips of leather. It was a sign of the leader's authority at ceremonies and identified him as the person to talk to when tribes met one another.

When people learned to make woven textiles, they added strips of dyed cloth to the staff. Dyed cloth could be made much larger and brighter than feathers and braided leather strips. Even better, the wind could make a cloth streamer stand out and flutter, which made an impressive sight. As time went on, the staff became merely the support for larger and larger pieces of cloth.

The Chinese, who invented silk cloth, made the first silk flags and perhaps the first flags of any material. Silk was an ideal material, sturdy but also lightweight, for flags. It takes only a light breeze to make a silk flag ripple beautifully. In both ancient China and India, flags were carried into battle on chariots.

The use of flags spread eastward to the Middle East. In the seventh and eighth centuries, when Muhammad and his Muslim followers began the Arab conquest of the Middle East, north Africa, and southern Europe, they rode with a black or

19

This knight on horseback proudly wears his coat of arms. From a Codex Emo-Capodilista manuscript.

white flag flying at the front. Their flag represented not just the ruler but also the people and their religion. Soldiers marching into battles were inspired by the flag flying at the head of their ranks. When the Muslim religion later split into several sects, the Fatimids flew green flags in honor of Muhammad's green cloak. Another sect, the Kharijites, carried red flags into battle. Because Islam prohibits the use of pictures and other visual symbols, these Islamic flags were solid color, with no emblems.

When the European Crusaders went to conquer Jerusalem from the Arabs about 1100, they returned with the Arab idea of flags. Unlike Arab flags, however, medieval European flags were elaborate. Heraldry (the art of designing and assigning a coats of arms to a family) was developing just at that time. A coat of arms was a collection of symbols and colors that people could "read" to understand a family's ideals. For example, gold signified the bearer's generosity; silver signified sincerity; green meant hope, joy, and loyalty in love; and red meant military strength. Castles, lions, plows, miters, and many other emblems told a family's history or occupation.

Medieval knights were the first to adopt coats of arms. They jousted in tournaments and rode into battles with their coat of arms stitched onto banners. Soon, not only knights but noble families, towns, religious orders, and guilds (organizations of people of the same profession) had banners bearing their coat of arms.

Over the centuries, many countries' flags have become simplified. The detailed emblems that adorned medieval flags have

Flags of all nations burst with color.

been eliminated. Flags with bold patterns of simple colors are easy to recognize and also easier to make in large quantities.

People are still very emotional about flags. When flags are raised behind the winners at the Olympic Games, the people of those countries may recall the good things and noble ideals their country stands for. Because flags have frequently been carried into battle, flags also recall those who died for their country.

More than 1.5 million Americans visit the U.S. Marine Corps War Memorial statue outside Washington, D.C., every year. The statue is based on a famous photograph of six American soldiers struggling to raise the American flag on Iwo Jima, a Japanese island where nearly seven thousand soldiers lost their lives during World War II. Flags, like uniforms and clothing, are just pieces of dyed cloth. However, the particular colors of those pieces of cloth speak clearly to us of strong emotions and ideas.

The colorful fabric used to wrap
this centuries-old Peruvian mummy is still intact.

CHAPTER TWO

The Ancient History
of Dyes

We take textiles (any material made from woven fibers) for granted, but textiles were a stunning invention about 6000 B.C. Before textiles, people wore animal hides, which they had learned to soften into leather. Textiles were more flexible and cooler than leather, and they were not as time consuming (and dangerous!) to obtain.

From the time people first wove textiles, they looked for ways to color them. They probably first tried to use the clay, chalk, and charcoal that they used to paint their bodies and cave walls. After the first washing or drenching in the rain, though, they would have discovered that most of these substances wash out of cloth. Most clays, chalks, and charcoal do not permanently penetrate the fibers of cloth. They are not dyes that permanently bind with cloth fibers.

Our knowledge of the earliest dyed textiles is limited. Over time, most textiles are destroyed by bacteria that eat the fibers. Unlike bones or metal or stone objects, textiles usually

In 6000 B.C., people around the world gathered much of their food from the forest or plains. They experimented with plants to figure out which roots, leaves, and berries tasted good, which couldn't be digested, and which cured ailments. People must have noticed that some pollens, petals, leaves, roots, and berries stained their clothes. We can guess that they tested these plant parts to see if they could permanently color cloth.

don't survive thousands of years to be found by archaeologists. Occasionally, however, special circumstances preserve scraps of fabric. When the ancient Egyptians wrapped mummies in colored linen, they first soaked the linen with the same chemicals that they used to preserve the bodies. The linen was further preserved by Egypt's hot, dry climate conditions. Archaeologists have found mummy wrappings in blue, yellow, and red that were woven and dyed about 3000 B.C.

Archaeologists in Scandinavia have found textiles preserved in the water-logged silt of bogs. Because there was no air deep in the bog, bacteria couldn't live and therefore didn't destroy the fabrics.

MAKING COLORS PERMANENT

Before people wove textiles out of wool, silk, or plants, they wore animal hides. An untreated animal hide makes very uncomfortable clothing. It is stiff and scratchy for a long time before oils from the wearer's skin soften it. Just about the time the hide softens, it wears out. People all over the world had good reason to search for ways to soften animal hides more quickly.

The ancient Egyptians discovered that alum, a mineral found in the ground and in certain plants, would soften hides.

In areas where oak trees grew (which included most of the areas bordering the Mediterranean Sea), people discovered that water in which oak bark and oak galls had soaked also softened hides. The bark and galls of oak trees contain tannic acid, which breaks down collagen, a protein that makes hides stiff. A hide is said to be tanned after it has been treated with alum, tannic acid, or similar substances.

Oak galls are the bumps that you see on oak trees. The female of certain flies and wasps makes a hole in the oak tree's bark and lays her eggs. When the larvae hatch, they feed on the tree and secrete a chemical irritant that makes the tree produce a growth around the larvae. The growth protects the tree from the insects and the insects from hungry birds. When the larvae mature into adults, they chew their way out of the gall.

Thousands of years ago when people first began weaving and dyeing cloth, they experimented with the same materials that softened and preserved leather. They had already noticed that tanned hides absorbed dyes much more readily than untanned hides. When they soaked cloth in alum or tannic acid, they also discovered that the colors were not only stronger and brighter, but that sometimes the colors were completely different.

Tannic acid and alum are just two of many *mordants* that dyers discovered to make dyes permanently color textiles and leathers. Mordants are chemicals that react with both the dye and the textile or leather and bind them together. (The word "mordant" comes from the Latin *mordere*, which means to bite into.) Dyers found other mordants, including vinegar, lime, stale urine, ammonia, iron and tin compounds, and cream of tartar. Dyes that require a mordant are called *indirect dyes*.

With constant experimentation, people found combina-

The word "fast" when used with dyes has nothing to do with speed. It comes from the word "fasten." Fast dyes are dyes that fasten well to cloth and resist fading.

tions of different mordants and dyes that produced a range of strong colors. Not all dyes were completely *fast* (permanent) to sunlight or to washing. Because most of the dyes used in ancient times were made from local plants, people often redyed their clothes if the color faded.

YELLOW

Look in your kitchen spice drawer to see if you have a bottle of turmeric. If you do, you have one of mankind's oldest yellow dyes. Turmeric is a spice often used in cooking in India that is made from the finely ground roots of the turmeric (*Curcuma*) plant. This yellow dye was (and is) easy to make. It is also a *direct dye*, which means you don't have to use a mordant with it.

In Asia and the Middle East, roots of the turmeric plant, petals of the safflower, and the stigmas (the slender stalks in the middle of a flower) from a crocus were popular yellow vegetable dyes. Early European

You can make your own turmeric dye at home. Put 1 cup (240 ml) of water in a pot. Stir in ½ teaspoon (2.5 ml) of turmeric. With an adult's help, bring the water to a simmer (not a full boil). Cut a few pieces of white wool yarn and drop them in the pot. Wait ten minutes, turn off the heat, and lift out the pieces of wool. Rinse them under the tap and pat them dry between two pieces of paper towel. The wool is permanently dyed!

You can make a yellow-green dye from sunflower heads, a bright yellow dye from another spice called marjoram, and a coppery yellow from a plant called broom sedge. At the back of this book, you'll find a list of books and Web sites that have dye recipes.

Crocus sativus

dyers frequently used two other wild plants, weld and dyer's broom, to dye wool yellow. The ancient Chinese used gardenia flowers to make yellow dye. In North America, the bark of the black oak, white ash, and the Osage orange tree as well as the roots of the barberry bush and the leaves of a plant called arsesmart (which is prickly), also produced yellows.

BLUE

The two most famous blue dyes, *woad* (which rhymes with road) and *indigo*, were also made

Saffron is made from the stigmas of the *Crocus sativus*. It is a direct dye, and so was one of the first dyes to be discovered. It takes more than four thousand stigmas to produce one ounce of saffron, which is why saffron is an expensive spice. It also explains why early dyers looked for other yellow dyes!

Baptisia tinctoria (wild indigo)

from plants. Both woad and indigo leaves contain a chemical called *indigofera*, although there is a lot more indigofera in indigo than in woad. Woad grows in Europe; indigo is native to India and Egypt. Woad and indigo belong to a third kind of dye, called *vat dyes*. Vat dyes are difficult and time consuming to prepare, but the dyes produce strong and permanent colors.

To make blue dye from woad or indigo leaves, dye makers soaked the leaves in a vat of water for several days until the leaves began to decompose, or rot. Then they stirred the dye liquid for hours until the decomposing leaves broke apart and a dark sediment collected at the bottom of the vat. Finally, they removed the sediment, dried it, and formed it into dark blue cakes about the size of hockey pucks. To use the dye later, a dyer dissolved the dye cakes in an alkaline solution, which was often stale urine. When the dye cakes

Before Robin Hood's Merry Men could dress in Lincoln Green, a dyer first dyed wool yellow with weld and then in woad for blue. Dyers in western Asia made green in a similar way. Unfortunately, the greens in some of the ancient carpets made in the region have become blue. The yellow dyes made from turmeric, saffron, and other plants have faded, but the blue indigo is still strong.

dissolved in the alkaline solution, the liquid was clear. The dyer dipped the cloth, which first turned yellow, then—as the cloth absorbed oxygen from the air—green, and finally blue.

PURPLE

The Phoenicians lived along the coast of what is today Lebanon in the Middle East. Their civilization reached its peak from about 1100 to 850 B.C. The Phoenicians were the most skilled seafarers the world had ever seen. They sailed across the Mediterranean and even into the Atlantic at a time when sailors from other countries wouldn't venture out of sight of land and the ocean was a terrifying place. The Phoenicians didn't invent the purple-red dye made from sea snails, but they made a rich living from dyeing cloth with it and trading the cloth, and many other goods, around the world.

The yellowish mucus of the sea snail that is used for dye is produced in a tiny

Buy some red cabbage (or ask the grocer if you can have a few of the loose leaves usually found in the bin) and you can make beautiful shades of blue dye. Put a few outer leaves in a pot of water. With an adult's help, simmer the leaves for about twenty minutes. Take the leaves out with a fork and put a few pieces of white wool yarn in the pot. It won't take long before they're dyed a beautiful blue.

Mordants have a vivid effect on cabbage dye. Pour about 2 cups (480 ml) of the liquid out of the pot and divide it among three smaller pots. Add about ½ teaspoon (2.5 ml) of alum to one, ½ teaspoon of cream of tartar to the second, and 1 teaspoon (5 ml) of vinegar to the third. (You can find alum and cream of tartar in the spice section at the grocery store.) Add white wool yarn, simmer for a few minutes, remove, and rinse. You'll see some beautiful new colors!

■ ■ ■

The astonishing color transformation involved in indigo dyeing led some people to think about color as magic. In fact, the mysteries of dyeing encouraged the ancient Egyptians and others to pursue alchemy, the pseudoscience of turning ordinary metals into gold. If yellow could transform itself to green and then blue, why shouldn't gray lead be turned into shining gold?

gland near the snail's neck. The mucus can be used as a direct dye. If it is squeezed directly onto cloth, it will color cloth purple as the mucus is exposed to air and light. The Phoenicians, however, didn't apply the mucus directly to cloth. If they had, the cloth would have become splotchy. Instead, they used it as a vat dye.

To produce the dye, dye makers cracked open the shells of the larger snails, removed the glands, and dropped them into the dye vat.

The Phoenicians called themselves Canaanites, but it was the Greek name for them that stuck. *Phoenicians* in Greek means "people of the land of red." Not only did the Phoenicians introduce the world to a fabulous color, but they contributed the letters of the Roman alphabet, which is still used in languages such as English, Spanish, and French. The Phoenicians also invented glass.

Sea snails were used to produce purple dye in ancient times.

They crushed smaller snails and added the whole snail to the vat. In both cases, the mucus and bits of snail decomposed into a smelly greenish solution. Various additional ingredients were added. Then the dye maker soaked the cloth in the solution. When the cloth emerged, it was green. As the dye reacted to the air, the cloth gradually changed to a shade of purple. The final color depended on the particular species of snail, the ingredients in the dye liquid, how long the cloth soaked, and how long it was exposed to sunlight.

The Phoenician dye makers mastered the secrets of the sea snail and built an industry on their knowledge. They imported linen and cotton from Egypt and dyed lengths of cloth in shades of purple that ranged from dark red to sky blue. The purplish red was the most valuable.

Over time, the Phoenicians founded colonies around the Mediterranean, and they passed their knowledge of purple dyeing to the Greeks and Romans. Purple-dyed cloth was recognized around the ancient world as a treasure equal to jewels and precious metals. When Alexander the Great conquered Persia in 333 B.C., one of the great prizes he took was 5,000 talents of purple cloth, which would be valued today at more than $68 million.

RED

People dyed textiles red with *madder* for thousands of years. Madder is a plant that grows wild throughout most of the world, but is especially abundant in Asia and Europe. The dye is in the roots of the plant. Madder colors

Purple was very expensive because it took thousands of sea snails to produce enough dye to color the cloth for one robe. The sea snails, which were trapped underwater in baited baskets, could only be harvested when the seas were calm.

wool easily and permanently, but its shades can be a bit dull. When used with alum and tin mordants, madder colors wool a range of tones including a ruddy brown, brick red, orange, coral, and pink.

Ancient dyers who wanted a brighter red dye than madder used kermes. Kermes dye was first made in India and Persia (modern Iran). For a long time—because kermes dyers were so secretive—Europeans didn't know that the dye was made from insects, and thought it was made from tiny berries.

Kermes dye was expensive (although not as expensive as purple) because the insects were only harvested once a year, and each insect produced only a tiny amount of dye. After the male insects impregnated the females in April, the males died. Just before the females were ready to lay their eggs in May, the harvesters collected them, using their fingernails, which some women grew long for the purpose. The kermes insects had to be harvested before daylight when the prickly leaves of the trees were still soft with dew. After the dye makers killed the insects with steam or by drowning, they dried them in the sun and ground them into powder. Kermes produced crimson, a deep red with blue tones.

COLOR BECOMES A BUSINESS

Thousands of years ago in the early days of textiles, people spun and wove their own cloth at home. They dyed the cloth at home, too, with dyes they made from plants they could gather in the surrounding countryside. They prepared the dyes according to recipes handed down from one generation to the next.

This illustration *from a ninth-century Italian manuscript depicts two men dyeing fabric. The artist was Rabanus Maurus (c. 780-856).*

Early in the first millennium B.C., even when people still wove their cloth at home, some people began to bring it to professional dyers for coloring. Professional dyers in towns around the Mediterranean Sea could afford to buy expensive dyes from traders who arrived by ship or caravan from around the world. They also had workshops with large pottery vats to store dye liquids, mordants, and water. Their most important assets, though, were the secret recipes for colors. Dyers held their secrets closely, rarely writing them down. There were fortunes to be made from these recipes.

Dyers in ancient Greece and Rome specialized in different colors and banded together in guilds for purple dyers, yellow dyers, red dyers, and the like. When archaeologists uncovered the remains of Pompeii, an Italian city covered in ash by the eruption of Mount Vesuvius in A.D. 79, they found several dye shops. Some dye vats still contained the dried remains of dyes, including purple and kermes red. Over the doorway of one shop was a carving of Mercury, the Roman god of commerce. In his hand, he held a bag of money, and above his head were carved the words *salve, lucrum*, meaning "welcome, profit." Dyeing had become big business.

CHAPTER THREE
What Are Dyes?

WHAT IS COLOR?

When you look at a piece of yarn dyed with turmeric, you see yellow. But what does that mean, to see yellow? What makes yellow look yellow?

When you see the yellow yarn, you are seeing light that has bounced off the yarn toward your eyes. Light, whether it comes from the sun or from a lamp, travels in waves, like waves moving across the surface of the ocean. Ocean waves are created by the energy of the blowing wind. Light waves are created by the energy of chemical reactions in the sun or by electrical energy flowing through a filament in a lightbulb.

The distance from the top of one wave to the top of the next wave—whether the waves are ocean waves or light waves—is called their wavelength. Every color in the rainbow (which is the spectrum of visible colors) has a different wavelength. Those wavelengths are measured in nanometers, which are billionths of a meter. Red light has the longest wave-

The spectrum *of light waves*

length, about 650 nanometers (30 millionths of an inch). Violet light has the shortest wavelength, about 470 nanometers (15 millionths of an inch). White light, like sunlight, is made up of light waves of every wavelength. You see white light when light of every color is present.

A yellow traffic light looks yellow because the glass in front of the bulb lets only yellow light waves (with a wavelength of about 570 nanometers, or about 25 millionths of an inch) pass through. All other wavelengths are blocked.

Without your eyes and your brain, you couldn't see color. Your eyes collect the light, and your brain interprets it. Your brain converts light of certain wavelengths into a perception of certain colors. Humans and other primates (such as monkeys, chimpanzees, and gorillas) see in color. So do fish, amphibians, some reptiles and birds, bees, and butterflies.

Yellow objects, like dyed cloth, however, look yellow for a different reason. The colors of objects that don't emit light are produced by a process called *color subtraction*. When white light hits dyed cloth, the light is either reflected or absorbed by *chromophores* in the dye. Chromophores are chemicals that absorb light of certain wavelengths. The wavelengths that the chromophores do not absorb are reflected back to the eye, and the viewer sees the remaining color. In other words, one color appears because other colors have been subtracted from the full spectrum in white light.

PAINTS AND DYES

Whether you are looking at a piece of canvas painted blue or a piece of canvas dyed blue, your eyes perceive blue in the same way. The painted or dyed cloth absorbs all colors, except blue, which it reflects. The ways that painted cloth and dyed cloth hold that color in place for your eyes to perceive, however, are different.

The color part of paints are *pigments*. Pigments are microscopic pieces of a colored material that are spread on the surface of an object. Pigments are bound tightly to surfaces by *binders*. The pigments in oil paints are bound to canvas with dried oil. Latex paints use plastics as binders. In the case of watercolors, the pigments are caught on the rough surfaces of the paper fibers when the water evaporates. Paints can be scraped off surfaces.

Dyes, on the other hand, actually become a part of the structure of the material that is dyed. They are chemically bonded to the material. There is no way to physically remove a dye—not even

During the Renaissance, which began in the 1300s in Italy, painters used ground-up lapis lazuli (a semiprecious gem) as a blue pigment in paint. Renaissance artists often charged an additional fee for a painting that included blue.

■ ■ ■

Some inks are paints and can be removed from writing surfaces. Medieval scribes often used a soot-based ink to write on parchment (a piece of animal hide that has been preserved, softened, and whitened). Parchment was expensive, and sometimes scribes would scrape off the ink of one document and write on it again. Scribes also used dyes as inks. The colored inks they used for the first capital letter in a document were often dyes.

by scraping or rubbing, for example. Each of the three kinds of dyes—direct, indirect, and vat dyes—use a different kind of chemical bond to attach to a material.

HOW DYES BOND TO TEXTILES

Elements are substances that are made of only one kind of atom. Carbon, oxygen, and hydrogen, for example, are elements. Dyes and textiles are made of chemical compounds. Compounds are substances made up of two or more elements chemically combined. Water, for example, is a compound. It is made of two atoms of hydrogen chemically combined with one atom of oxygen.

An atom is made of three smaller particles: protons, neutrons, and electrons. At the center of an atom is a cluster of protons and neutrons called the nucleus. Protons carry a positive (+) electrical charge. Neutrons are electrically neutral and carry no charge. Electrons, much smaller than protons or neutrons, carry a negative (−) electrical charge. In uncharged or neutral atoms, the number of

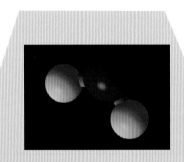

Model of a water molecule

Chemists use abbreviations and symbols for elements and compounds. H is the abbreviation for hydrogen. O is the abbreviation for oxygen. The symbol for the compound water is H_2O: two hydrogen atoms combined with one oxygen atom.

positively charged protons in the nucleus is equal to the number of negatively charged electrons circling them.

Electrons are in motion, orbiting the nucleus in unpredictable patterns. Why don't electrons fly off, away from the nucleus? It is the attraction between the positive protons and the negative electrons that keeps the electrons in orbit. According to modern atomic theory, electrons circle the nucleus in unpredictable patterns, but at particular distances from the nucleus, according to how much energy an electron possesses. Each particular distance can hold only a certain number of electrons. You can picture these specific distances as shells surrounding the nucleus. The innermost shell can hold two electrons, the second shell can hold up to eight, and the third shell can hold up to eight (or eighteen in the heavier elements).

The electron shells of an atom fill up with electrons from the innermost shell to the outermost. A neutral sodium atom (Na), for example, has eleven protons and eleven electrons. The innermost shell is filled with two electrons. The second shell is filled up with eight. In the third, outermost shell, there is one electron. Electrons in the outermost shell are called valence electrons. The valence electrons are very important in determining how dyes stick to textiles.

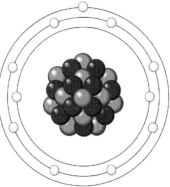

Model of
a sodium atom

Atoms that have completely filled outermost shells are stable. They usually do not combine with other atoms to form compounds. Atoms whose outermost shells are not complete form chemical bonds more easily. There is a tendency for atoms to achieve stability by either gaining, losing, or sharing electrons so that their outermost shells will be complete.

DIRECT DYES

If a sodium atom loses its single valence electron from its third shell, it will be stable. This electron is easily stripped from sodium. Fluorine (F) is an element with seven valence electrons. An atom of fluorine will achieve stability if it gains one electron in its outermost shell. Under the right conditions, when an atom of sodium comes in contact with an atom of fluorine, the sodium atom loses its one valence electron to the fluorine atom. Both are now stable with their outermost shells filled up.

But what about the electrical charges of the atoms? Are they still neutral? The answer is no. The sodium atom has the same eleven protons, but now has only ten electrons. It has a small positive charge. A sodium atom that has lost its valence electron is called a sodium ion. The fluorine atom is also charged. It has the same nine protons, but now it has ten electrons. The fluorine ion has a small negative charge. Chemists abbreviate the sodium ion as Na+, which means the sodium atom has one more proton than it does

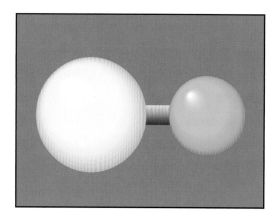

Model of sodium fluoride

electrons. The chemical abbreviation for the fluorine ion is F−, which means the fluorine atom has one more electron than it does protons.

Because opposite charges attract, the positive sodium ion is attracted to the negative fluorine ion. The attraction is similar to the way the south end of one magnet pulls toward the north end of another. This attachment between sodium and fluorine is called an ionic bond. Once the sodium and fluorine are bonded, the new chemical substance is called sodium fluoride.

Dyes are complex compounds made of many elements. Direct dyes, such as turmeric, bond to textiles with ionic bonds. A negatively charged element in the dye compound is attracted to a positively charged element in the compounds that make up the textile.

In another kind of chemical bonding called covalent bonding, atoms do not lose or gain electrons, but share them. The formation of a water molecule (H_2O) is a good example of covalent bonding. Oxygen has eight protons and eight electrons. Two electrons complete the inner shell of oxygen, leaving six electrons in the outer shell. Oxygen tends to achieve stability by completing its outer shell with two electrons. Hydrogen has one proton and one electron. Oxygen joins with two hydrogen atoms, so that the electron from each hydrogen atom becomes a part of oxygen's outermost shell, making it stable. The hydrogen atoms also achieve stability because they have two electrons in their outermost shell. When oxygen bonds with a pair of hydrogen atoms, the H_2O molecule results.

INDIRECT DYES

Indirect dyes require a mordant to attach to textiles. A mordant contains positively charged ions of a metallic element. Aluminum (Al) ions, chromium (Cr) ions, copper (Cu) ions, iron(Fe) ions, and tin (Sn) ions are commonly used mordants.

When a dyer soaks a textile in a mordant, the positively charged mordant forms an ionic bond with negatively charged elements in the textile.

When the dyer then soaks the mordanted textile in the dye, the mordant also bonds in a similar way with the dye. The mordant becomes a bridge, linking the dye to the textile.

VAT DYES

A vat dye, such as indigo, bonds with textiles in a different way. Indigo is a pigment that does not dissolve in water. It does, however, dissolve in the presence of an alkali. Alkalis are metals whose atoms have a single electron in their outermost shells. Sodium and potassium are alkalis. Dyers often dissolve indigo in urine because urine is rich in potassium.

After dissolving the indigo in a vat filled with an alkali liquid, the dyer added the textile. The textile fibers absorbed the dye liquid. At first, the textile was yellow like the dye liquid. The color only gradually appeared as blue when the dyer removed the textile and let it dry. At this point it became permanently dyed.

Alkalis bond with elements that need an electron to complete their outermost shells. The most familiar alkali compound is ordinary salt, which is a compound of sodium (Na) and chlorine (Cl) ions. Sodium is an alkali metal. It has one electron in its outermost shell. Chlorine has seven electrons in its outermost shell. Sodium and chlorine bond to form the compound NaCl. Other familiar alkali compounds are soaps and baking soda.

44

What happened? As the textile dried in the air, the dye molecules combined with oxygen in the air and became bits of insoluble (not dissolvable) blue pigment again. But now the dye molecules were inside the textile, physically trapped inside the core of the textile fibers. Textile fibers formed cages around the indigo molecules and trapped them.

Blue jeans are vat dyed with synthetic indigo. You may see the words "stonewashed" on some blue jeans. Stonewashed blue jeans are literally washed with stones in industrial-sized washing machines until the jeans fade.

SYNTHETIC DYES

As you will see in Chapter Five, *synthetic* (man-made) *dyes* have largely replaced natural dyes like turmeric and indigo. The chemistry of synthetic dyes is much the same as the chemistry of natural dyes. In fact, it was chemists' gradual understanding of the chemical processes at work in making natural dyes that led them to invent synthetic dyes.

These shoes are made *from synthetically dyed canvas.*

In this French painting by *Louis Le Nain*
(ca. 1593–1648) called Return from Baptism, *the peasants
are wearing the drab clothing typical of the times.*

CHAPTER FOUR

From Kermes to Cochineal

DYES IN THE MIDDLE AGES

After the fall of the Roman Empire about A.D. 500, there was little communication between western Europe and the Middle East and Asia. Barbarian tribes from central Europe and Scandinavia migrated west and south, conquering as they went and disrupting the societies and economies of the lands they invaded. Travel within western Europe was difficult and dangerous because the old Roman roads fell into disrepair and "highway robbers" attacked travelers with no fear of arrest. Trade within Europe declined dramatically. Trade with the East—where many of the most beautiful dyes, such as saffron, indigo, purple from sea snails, kermes, and purple and red from brazilwood were grown or harvested—nearly ceased. Only small amounts of the dyes and the beautiful dyed silks made in the East were shipped to western Europe, and these were so expensive only nobility could afford them.

In this engraving of a medieval French cloth factory, two dyers, wearing wooden clogs and protective clothing, use long poles to push cloth into a vat of dye.

The cities of Tyre and Sidon, once the principal cities of the Phoenician Empire, were conquered by the Greeks, the Romans, and the Persians. The dye works in these cities continued to produce purple under their new rulers. The Greeks and Romans also developed their own purple dye industries, but these closed during the turmoil caused by the fall of the Roman Empire and the invasions from the north. The dye works in Tyre and Sidon finally closed when the Arabs conquered Tyre in the seventh century.

By the ninth century, the only purple dye works left were in Constantinople, and those were controlled the Byzantine emperor. Purple became rarer and more expensive than ever. When Constantinople fell to the Ottoman Turks in 1453, the last purple dye works in the world ceased to exist. Because purple dyers always kept their ingredients and processes secret, when the last dye works closed, the ancient secret of dyeing Tyrian purple with sea snails was lost.

As a result, during the first part of the Middle Ages (roughly 500 to 1000) many peasants in western Europe wore clothes made of undyed gray linen and undyed beige or brown wool. When they dyed cloth, people relied on local plants, such as madder, weld, and woad. These plants could produce bright colors (although not as bright as kermes or modern synthetic dyes). However, early medieval dyers often used cloth that was not well bleached or mordanted, and the results were usually more muted shades, such as brick reds, muddy yellows, and grayish blues.

A TURNING POINT

The economies of western Europe were ravaged for hundreds of years by barbarian invasions from central Europe, Muslim invasions from the south, Viking invasions from Scandinavia, and Magyar invasions from the east. For centuries, trade was nearly nonexistent and money virtually disappeared. When crops were bad or ruined by invaders, peasants starved.

By 1000, however, many of the barbarian invaders had become assimilated into the European duchies, kingdoms, and other states that were slowly developing in western Europe. By 1100 the Christian states in northern Spain were pushing out the Muslims, who had held most of the Iberian Peninsula. Across Europe, wealthier, more powerful rulers were restoring order.

Political stability encouraged farmers to clear new land and to take advantage of new technology, such as heavy plows and iron horseshoes. European farmers produced more grain and were able to raise more livestock for food and for wool. Farmers produced more than they needed and had a surplus they could trade for products made by local and foreign crafts-men. Trade revived, and merchants built newer and bigger ships to carry the larger shipments across the Mediterranean.

Starting in 1095, the first of tens of thousands of European Crusaders traveled through Constantinople on their way to conquer Jerusalem from the Arabs. The Crusaders were aston-ished by the richly colored silk velvets, brocades, and damasks they saw in the East. After living in a world of undyed or badly dyed wool and linen clothing, they were delighted with the wide range of colors and the luxurious fabrics. They bought—or more often looted—them and brought them back home. Their countrymen were awed by these and other eastern goods, and soon developed a yen for colored eastern fabrics.

Constantinople and especially Venice (a Mediterranean island city-state in northern Italy) became wealthy acting as middlemen between western merchants selling wool, tin, and other commodities and eastern merchants offering silk, car-pets, spices, and dyes. Venice also became a great textile cen-ter. Venetian merchants imported wool from northern Europe and silk from the East, wove it and dyed it, and exported it throughout the world. They also developed a lucrative business making red caps called fezzes, which many men in the Byzantine Empire wore. Venice's dyers helped make Venice the most prosperous and powerful city in late medieval Europe.

Beautifully colored silk clothing made in the East became popular among the wealthy western Europeans. As the European economies revived, people of less exalted rank, too, could afford dyed linen cloth, at least for special occasions. At the coronation of King Louis VIII of France in 1223, chroni-

During the Middle Ages, Venice was a great textile center where merchants hawked their wares, as this Italian miniature painted in 1470 shows.

There was a long-standing rivalry between Constantinople and Venice for the lucrative East-West trade. In 1204, Crusaders from western Europe arrived in Venice, on their way to Jerusalem. Venetian political leaders managed to convince the Crusaders (who were in desperate need of money) to attack and sack Constantinople. With Constantinople's defeat, Venice became the primary entrepôt (center for trade) between East and West.

Venetians became expert dyers. The dyers were organized into powerful guilds, which specialized in particular colors. Those who dyed with "Venetian scarlet," a dye made from a secret recipe that involved mordanting kermes in alum and tartar, maintained the high quality of their dye by regulating its production. One regulation, for example, prohibited any dyer from adding brazilwood, a cheaper but less permanent red dye made from trees, to kermes. Dyers who cheated could be punished by having a hand cut off!

clers reported that all classes of society wore brightly colored fine linens and wools.

NEW WORLD DYES

In 1519—only twenty-seven years after Columbus first brought the New World to the attention of Europe— Hernando Cortés and a contingent of about six hundred Spanish soldiers began a two-year conquest of Mexico. Cortés and his band looted gold, found extensive silver mines, and soon discovered a very interesting insect in southern Mexico that the Aztecs and other native tribes used to make a red dye.

They called the insect "cochinilla," which was translated as *cochineal* (*KOH-chih-neel*) in English. Cochineal insects are tiny round parasites that live almost exclusively on the opuntia (prickly pear) cactus. The female insects produce a dye when they are pregnant, an event that occurs three times a year

Cochineal insects on the spiny pad of a prickly pear cactus can be harvested and crushed to produce a red dye.

under ideal conditions. After the native farmers harvested the insects by brushing them off the cacti with a feather or a deer's tail, they dried them in the sun or in ovens.

The Spanish explorers sent dyed cloth and dried insects back to Spain, where dyers discovered that the cochineal dye was ten times stronger than kermes dye. "Send more cochineal," was the message from Spain, and so the settlers encouraged the native Mexicans to grow and pick more and more cochineal. By the late 1500s, cochineal had become the third most valuable export from the Spanish colonies, after gold and silver. The English, French, and Dutch pirates who preyed on the semiannual *flota*, the large group of cargo ships that sailed from the colonies to Spain, were just as happy to take a ship laden with cochineal as with silver.

France was paying so much gold to Spain for cochineal that one intrepid, patriotic French botanist decided he would try to steal the live insects for France. In 1777, Thierry de Menonville, botanist to King Louis XVI, set sail for Oaxaca *(Wa-HA-ka)*, the center of cochineal farming, in New Spain. He made it as far as the walled city of Vera Cruz, the major port of New Spain, but then the suspicious Spanish viceroy ordered him out on the next ship. Instead of complying, Thierry scaled the walls, disguised himself as a Catalonian physician looking for herbal medicines, and set out on foot for Oaxaca, about 125 miles (200 kilometers) away.

Thierry tricked a monk into giving him a map, dodged Spanish soldiers, and bought cacti and live cochineal bugs from unsuspecting farmers. Then he purchased boxes for the insect-infested cacti and hid the cacti among many other specimens he collected. He managed to return to Vera Cruz, where he boarded a ship bound for the French colony of Haiti. The ship he took was caught in terrible storms, and most of his plants and insects died. When he reached Haiti, however, he had enough left to start his own cochineal plantation.

Spain was determined to keep the great profits from this valuable dye to itself. The Spanish government forbade the export of live cochineal, and foreigners were forbidden from traveling inland in New Spain (as Mexico was called) for fear they would steal it. The Spanish even managed to keep the secret of what exactly cochineal was, pretending that it was the seed or fruit of a plant, until the eighteenth century.

The discovery of cochineal, which was more potent and cheaper than kermes, contributed to the decline of Venice and the rise of Spain as an international economic force. Dyers around the world, as far away as China, turned to Spain for bright red dye. In Britain, the army had its officers' uniforms dyed with cochineal. In the United States, Betsy Ross used cochineal-dyed cloth for her flag. Clothing, draperies, and upholstery were dyed cochineal red.

Betsy Ross making the American flag by
Jean Leon Jerome Ferris (1863–1930)

The color that was once the province of the wealthy became more widely available.

The New World was rich in dyestuffs that Europeans and European colonists gathered or cultivated with profit. In the Middle Ages, people had found another red from brazilwood growing in India. In the sixteenth century, when the Portuguese sailors found it growing profusely in South America, they named the country Brazil for the dye. In Central America, the Spanish also harvested logwood, which produced dyes from dark blue to purple to black.

A variety of the indigofera plant was native to many regions in the Americas, and the Spanish reported that natives dyed their bodies and faces blue with it. During the sixteenth and seventeenth centuries, the British, French, and Germans all passed laws forbidding the use of indigo (known in parts of Germany as "devil's dye"), both from India and the Americas. In the eighteenth century, however, the British government gave up the fight against the superior dye and promoted the cultivation of indigo in its North and South Carolina colonies. Indigo became a major export crop of the southern colonies in the United States.

The Spanish colonists virtually enslaved Native Mexicans to work in the gold and silver mines. They also took over huge tracts of land in northern Mexico. In contrast, many Native Mexicans in southern Mexico benefited from the Spanish presence. The Spanish discovered that only native peoples, mostly Mixtecs and Zapotecs, could profitably grow and harvest the cochineal. The Spanish left the native farmers of Oaxaca to produce the crop in their small backyard plots and made their profit by shipping the crop to Spain for sale. Oaxaca became the wealthiest region in New Spain.

CHAPTER FIVE

From Madder to Mauve

MADDER

On May 20, 1498, Portuguese sea captain Vasco da Gama landed in India near the town of Calicut. He was the first of many Europeans who would arrive by sea in the following centuries, sailing around the Cape of Good Hope at the southern tip of Africa. Da Gama and his successors from Portugal, France, Holland, and England came to buy or trade for the beautiful cotton fabrics, indigo, and spices that were made or grown in India and Asia.

Da Gama's discovery of the sea route changed the economies of the Old World. The exotic Asian and Indian goods that had trickled by overland caravan to Constantinople and Venice along the Silk Route were suddenly available in the large quantities that ships could hold. Although the ocean voyages were perilous, sending goods by ship was a cheaper and safer method than sending them by land.

Calicut was a city already famous for what the English would call "calicut" or, more often, calico cloth. Calico was a

Overland traders from India and Asia had to pay taxes, or duties, at every one of the many borders they crossed, and they ran a constant risk of robbery. On the ocean, there were no border crossings. Although pirates hunted the seas for merchant ships, a ship was much more likely to pass undetected on the trackless ocean than a wagon on one of the few roads across Europe.

cotton fabric that was painted or printed with designs in two or more bright, fast colors. Deep blue from indigo and a bright red from madder were the most popular calico colors. When da Gama arrived, the Indians had already been cultivating and weaving cotton for 4,500 years and had supplied white cotton cloth to the ancient Egyptians, Chinese, Greeks, and Romans. Indian dyers had been making and trading the colorful calicoes for at least 1,500 years.

For most Europeans of the late Middle Ages, cut off from trade with the East, cotton was a new textile and calico was a great novelty. Cotton won't grow in the cool climate of northern Europe, and European wool cloth couldn't be printed with patterns. Europeans were familiar with plaids and stripes woven into woolens, but cotton fabric patterned with exotic multicolored flowers, winding vines, curved shapes called paisleys, and stylized animals was a novelty. Europeans were enchanted with the finely woven and beautifully dyed calico. They were also delighted to have a fabric that was cool in the summer and that, unlike wool, could be easily washed.

Calicoes imported from India became a fashion craze of the upper classes in Europe in the 1660s and 1670s. Wealthy and well-born English, French, German, and Dutch women snapped up the expensive calicoes when they arrived by ship

In this seventeenth-century Italian painting
by an anonymous artist, a woman wears a dress made of cloth
patterned with paisleys.

from India. Never before had a fashion swept across international borders in this way.

European entrepreneurs saw an opportunity. They had been importing white Indian cotton fabrics as well as weaving a mixture of linen and cotton (called *fustian*) for several decades. Now, cotton and fustian printers opened shop with inexpensive copies, also called calicoes, of the Indian imports. The European printers were able to reproduce blue with either woad or indigo, but red was a problem. Neither cochineal nor kermes worked well on cotton. European madder recipes produced only a dull brick-red color. Dyers in India, Turkey, and Greece were able to use madder to dye a bright red color called "Turkey red" on cotton, but they kept the recipe a secret.

These European calicoes were eagerly purchased by women who couldn't afford the more brightly colored Indian calicoes. Calicoes, both imported and European-made, became so popular that owners of the French, English, and German wool cloth factories of northern Europe and their workers felt endangered. European governments were also alarmed at how much gold and silver were leaving the country to pay for the Indian imports. In 1686 the French banned calicoes, and soon after the English and Germans enacted similar laws.

The bans on calico only increased the demand for the cloth. You've seen what happens when there isn't enough of a popular toy on the store shelves. Somehow, the fact that a toy is in short supply makes it even more desirable. The same thing happened in the late seventeenth and early eighteenth centuries with adults and calicoes.

Although the French cotton printers were forced to close down, they moved to Holland and Switzerland, where they could work legally. Smugglers supplied French, English, and German women who were willing to risk stiff fines for buying or wearing calico. In France, the police tore the calicoes off the backs of women caught wearing them, and officials publicly burned calico garments. Calico smugglers were sometimes sentenced to death.

It took at least a month to dye cotton with Turkey red. The cloth or thread was first prepared by bleaching several times, oiling, and soaking in cow or sheep manure. Then it was soaked in tannic acid. Mordanting was next, using alum and cream of tartar or arsenic and carbonate of soda (depending on the desired shade of red). Vigorous washing followed. Next, the cloth was boiled in a dye bath of madder mixed with ox or sheep blood. Finally, the cloth was rinsed and washed with soap and spread out to dry in the sun.

Finally, in the 1740s the French ban was relaxed and then eliminated altogether in 1759. Calico factories sprang up in Marseilles in southern France and then elsewhere in France. Now calico printers could turn their attention to making a bright red. French industry spies traveled to Greece to steal the secret of Turkey red. Some of these adventurers came home with the complex recipes that eastern dyers used. It took more than a copy of a recipe, however, to make Turkey red dye. The eastern ingredients were different or unavailable in the West. Dyers found that substituting European linseed oil, for example, for rancid Greek olive oil darkened the final color. In addition, the type of madder grown in the Middle East was not the same as the madder grown in France.

In the mid-1700s, French entrepreneurs managed to entice some Greek dyers of Turkey red to France to help them adapt their recipes to western European conditions and ingredients. The French cotton printers managed to keep the secret of Turkey red for awhile, but the English and Scots soon learned it, too. When French scientist Jean Antoine Chaptal published his book *The Art of Dyeing Cotton* around 1800, the secret became available to all.

MAUVE

One evening in the spring of 1856, an eighteen-year-old chemistry student named William Perkin was working in the makeshift laboratory he had set up on the top floor of his small home in London. He was heating a glass container partly filled with a thick, black, oily tar. He hoped to transform the tar into synthetic quinine, a medicine for malaria.

In the 1850s, malaria infected thousands of people in England every year, and millions around the globe. No one knew what caused the disease, but people had known for hundreds of years that the roots and bark of the South American cinchona tree was a remedy. In 1820 two French

Since about 1800, Londoners had lit their homes, streets, and factories with a gas made from coal. The tar that Perkin was experimenting with was a small bit of the tons of tar waste from coal gasification. Inventors had discovered a few uses for the tar by mid-century. Charles Macintosh had invented raincoats (popularly known as mackintoshes) by coating cloth with rubber dissolved in naphtha, which is made from coal tar.

pharmacists isolated the essential ingredient, quinine, in cinchona bark. Quinine was expensive, however, and scarce, and the demand for it exceeded the supply. So when Perkin's chemistry professor suggested that coal tar might be changed by chemical means into quinine, Perkin decided to try.

Chemists of the 1850s, as we saw in Chapter Three, had identified more than sixty chemical elements, and they were aware of some of the properties of those elements. They had some understanding of atoms and knew that the atoms of certain elements joined together in predictable proportions to form compounds. What they didn't know was what caused the elements to bond together. So, when chemists wanted to alter a compound and change the ratio of elements in it, they performed traditional operations such as distillation and oxidization (adding oxygen and removing hydrogen), and simply hoped for success. Most often the experiments failed, but sometimes a chemist was lucky and his experiment worked.

Quinine is a clear substance, and when Perkin experimented on the coal tar that evening, he got a reddish powder. Many other chemists might have thrown away the powder—it certainly didn't look like quinine—and started over. Perkin didn't. He subjected the red powder to further chemical procedures, and transformed the powder into a black goo. Instead of tossing out this even more unlikely substance, he experimented further. He separated the components of the black substance and dried them out. When he combined one of the components with alcohol, he found it produced a beautiful bluish-purple color. When he dipped a scrap of silk in the water, the silk became bluish purple, too, and the color wouldn't wash out.

Perkin had accidentally made a synthetic dye. He called the color he made "mauve" (*mohv*) and called his dye *mauveine* (*moh-VEEN*). Other chemists had made synthetic dyes before: Picric acid dyed cloth yellow, and carbolic acid dyed cloth red. These dyes were curiosities, however, and their inventors never tried to produce them in quantity or sell them as dyes. No one before Perkin had ever seen any potential for a synthetic dye.

For awhile, Perkin was the only one interested in his mauve dye. He perfected the production process and took samples to cotton printers and dyers in England and Scotland. The cotton printers were not at all interested. Eventually, he convinced one London dyer to buy mauve and, with his father and brother, built a factory to produce it. Still, at the end of 1857, all he had was one customer and the large debts from building a factory.

In 1858, Perkin got lucky. Empress Eugénie, wife of the French emperor Napoleon III and a woman whose great fondness for clothes was matched by a large fortune with which to buy them, was seen wearing mauve-colored dresses. Then England's Queen Victoria, who probably looked to the more fashion-conscious Eugénie as a guide, wore a mauve velvet dress to her daughter's wedding. Suddenly, mauve was *the* fashionable color. Men wore mauve-colored waistcoats. Mauveine colored nearly every article of women's attire, from bonnets and parasols to shoes.

By 1860, at the age of twenty-two, Perkin had made a fortune with mauve. In rapid order, other chemists ran their own

Princess Eugénie wears a fashionable mauve dress in this oil on canvas painting by Franz Xavier Winterhalter (1806–1873).

experiments, and soon chemical factories in France, England, and Germany were producing a rainbow of synthetic colors, all from napthalene, an ingredient of coal tar. A French firm made magenta, which was bought in great quantity for soldiers' uniforms for warring armies in central Europe. Other firms turned out yellow and a number of blues, as well as green and new purples. Perkin's factory produced greens, pinks, and black. These colors had names like rosaniline, fuchsin, aniline yellow, and aldehyde green.

By the late 1860s, mauve was out of fashion and the price (and therefore the profits) of magenta had fallen considerably. Perkin turned his attention to bright red. Madder and cochineal were still the dyes of choice for a true scarlet, and naphthalene had yet to yield the color.

Perkin began experiments to reproduce the active ingredient of madder, alizarin. He worked with benzene, another ingredient of coal tar. Although he didn't know it, three chemists at the German firm BASF, Carl Graebe, Carl Liebermann, and an old friend and student of Perkin's, Heinrich Caro, were also working with benzene to make alizarin. The German team patented a process for making synthetic alizarin one day before the English patent office, after bureaucratic delays, issued a similar patent to Perkin.

The bright red alizarin was the next big color and created another small fortune for Perkin (who, in an agreement with BASF, got the British market) and a much larger one for BASF. After a German company synthesized indigo in 1880, German firms dominated the international dye market, producing 80 percent of the world's dyes by 1914.

Consumers loved synthetic dyes. They could be made in an endless range of colors and they were fast. Many dyers were also pleased with synthetic dyes because they were more likely to yield consistent colors than natural dyes. Natural dyes could be unpredictable because the quantity and quality of the dye varied plant by plant. Clothing manufacturers were happy, too. Synthetic dyes were cheaper than natural dyes, which meant clothes were cheaper and people could afford to buy more of them.

Synthetic dyes were important in themselves, but they proved to have a larger significance. Germany trained thousands of chemists in the dye industry, and those chemists went on to use their knowledge and skills in creating antiseptics, medicines, and other useful chemical compounds. When World War I broke out in 1914, the Germans were far ahead in chemical production.

What was good for synthetic dye manufacturers, chemists, consumers, and clothing manufacturers, however, was disastrous for natural dye producers. Natural dye producers had to lower the prices of their dyes to meet the competition from synthetic dyes. The natural dye business was suddenly no longer profitable. Madder, cochineal, indigo, and many other natural dye growers went out of business.

This modern-day Navajo rug weaver uses
yarns dyed with natural dyes.

Today, almost all fabric is dyed with synthetic dyes. Natural dyes, though, are still grown and used on a small scale. Small-scale weavers often use natural dyes, admiring their gentler tones and treasuring the variability of the colors they produce. You can grow and make many of the natural dyes or buy them at stores catering to weavers or through the Internet.

Ever since people learned to make textiles, we have wanted to color our clothes. We have always coveted dyes, whether natural or synthetic, as a way to communicate, and for thousands of years our desire for dyes has created rich industries around the world. Phoenicia made a fortune with its purple-red, Venice profited from kermes, and India and Spain grew rich from indigo and cochineal. After Perkin invented mauve, huge industries sprang up, primarily in Europe and later the United States, to manufacture dozens, hundreds, and eventually thousands of synthetic colors. Some of the biggest names in the European industry—BASF, Bayer, and Hoechst, for example—started by making synthetic dyes.

For thousands of years, dyed cloth has communicated ideas about religion, nationality, and social status. Today, it is hard to imagine dressing in your family's heraldic colors. Can you imagine being prohibited by law from wearing purple or red? Still, dyed cloth communicates ideas: In the United States, brides still wear white, mourners still wear black,

Today, many of the packaged foods we eat—from ketchups to cereals—are colored with dyes. Toothpastes, medicines, and other things we consume are also colored with food dyes. Many of the food dyes that manufacturers add are natural. For example, beet juice and the spice paprika are popular natural dyes that make food and other products red or pink.

In the nineteenth century, manufacturers added arsenic and other dangerous chemicals to color candies and brighten pickles. People were sickened and even died from eating food colored with these dyes. Today the U.S. Food and Drug Administration (FDA) administers a number of laws that regulate the use of synthetic colors in foods, drugs, and cosmetics. The FDA certifies that particular dyes are safe and gives them a number to indicate that they are approved. Only seven synthetic dyes are legal in the United States today: Yellows #5 and #6, reds #3 and #40, blues #1 and #2, and green #3. Take a look at the label on a toothpaste tube or a ketchup bottle to see what dyes are used to make them bright.

Today's athletes enjoy wearing bright colors.

and we dress baby girls in pink. Sports fans wear their team's colors to the stadium. The red, white, and blue of the American flag can still stir patriotic feelings.

Now, we use dyed cloth to express ourselves as individuals in a way our ancestors would never have imagined. In the twenty-first century, synthetic dyes allow you to wear any color in the rainbow—as well as iridescent and fluorescent colors never found there—just to please yourself.

Today, we dye much more than cloth. Dyes are used to color our food, our hair, and our lips. They are used to color a host of everday products from plastic furniture and toys to tape cassettes and school supplies. They are used in medicines, scientific research, and are important in projects for identifying microscopic particles.

Our world is filled with color—in part because of the miracle of dyes.

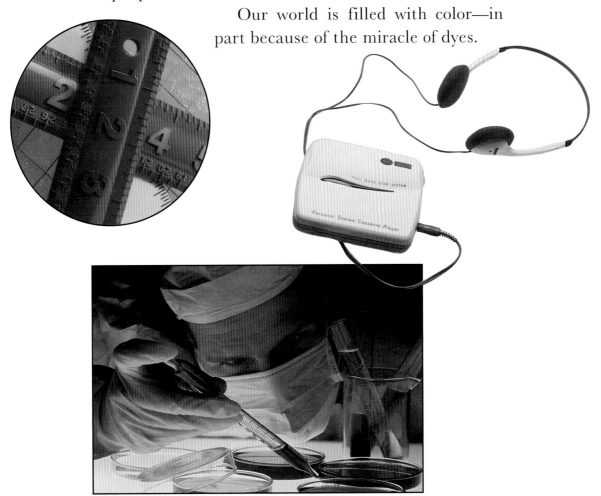

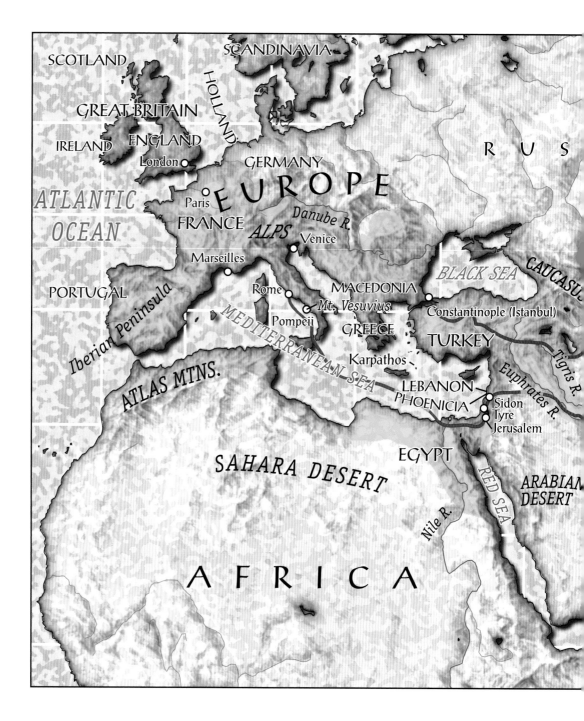

SCOTLAND

SCANDINAVIA

HOLLAND

GREAT BRITAIN

IRELAND

ENGLAND

London

GERMANY

EUROPE

R U S

ATLANTIC
OCEAN

Paris

FRANCE

ALPS

Danube R.

Venice

Marseilles

BLACK SEA

CAUCASU

PORTUGAL

Iberian Peninsula

Rome

MACEDONIA

Constantinople (Istanbul)

ATLAS MTNS.

MEDITERRANEAN SEA

Mt. Vesuvius

Pompeii

GREECE

Karpathos

TURKEY

Euphrates R.

Tigris R.

LEBANON
PHOENICIA

Sidon
Tyre
Jerusalem

SAHARA DESERT

EGYPT

RED SEA

ARABIAN
DESERT

Nile R.

A F R I C A

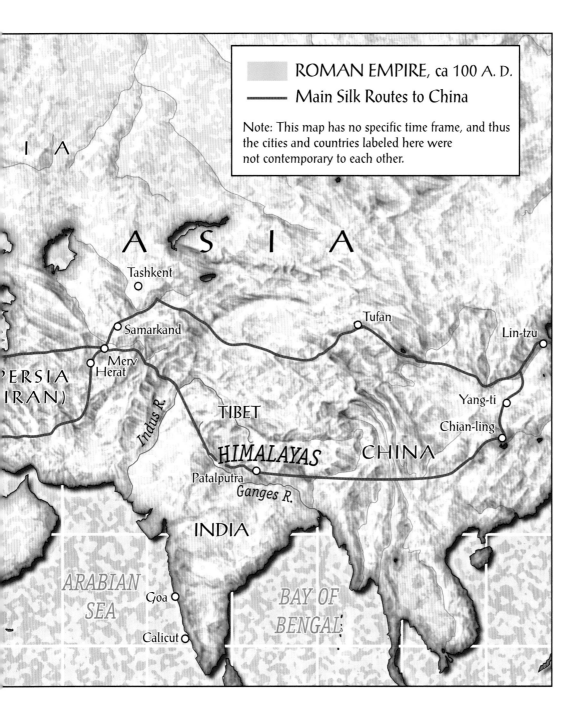

ROMAN EMPIRE, ca 100 A. D.

Main Silk Routes to China

Note: This map has no specific time frame, and thus the cities and countries labeled here were not contemporary to each other.

A S I A

Tashkent

Samarkand

Merv
Herat

PERSIA
(IRAN)

Indus R.

TIBET

HIMALAYAS

Patalputra
Ganges R.

INDIA

ARABIAN
SEA

Goa

Calicut

BAY OF
BENGAL

Tufan

Lin-tzu

Yang-ti

Chian-ling

CHINA

Timeline

B.C.

6000	Stone Age people begin experimenting with ways to dye cloth
3000	Egyptians dye wrappings for mummies
1000	Professional dyers emerge throughout the Mediterranean
1200	Phoenicians excel in making red dye from the mucus of sea snails
46	Julius Caesar begins to restrict the wearing of purple in Rome

A.D.

400s	Roman Empire falls
604	Twelve-Cap Ranking System, which identified a person's rank by the color of his cap, established in Japan
600s–700s	Arabs use flags in battle to represent people and their religion
800s	Constantinople becomes important dye manufacturing center
1095	First of the Crusaders exposed to richly colored fabrics of the East

1100 Heraldry develops in Europe; knights begin to wear colorful coats of arms

1204 Crusaders sack Constantinople, and Venice becomes primary entrepôt between East and West

1223 All classes of society wear brightly colored linens and wools at coronation of King Louis VIII of France

1328 France passes a law allowing princes and knights to wear scarlet

1400s Scarlet becomes a color of kings; in Scotland, working people limited to gray and white on working days

1453 Turks conquer Byzantine Empire; secret of making purple dye from snails is lost

1464 The pope decrees that cardinals will wear "cardinal's purple" robes dyed red with kermes

1519 Spaniards discover how Indians in Oaxaca, Mexico, make red dye from cochineal insects

1660s–1670s Indian calicoes become a fashion craze in Europe

1686–1759 Calicoes banned in France

1800 Jean Antoine Chaptal publishes *The Art of Dyeing Cotton*

1800s Men use silver nitrate-based formulas to darken their mustaches and hair

1850 Levi Strauss uses indigo to dye the first blue jeans

1856 William Perkin accidentally discovers how to make a synthetic dye he calls mauveine

1909 Eugene Schuller develops new kind of hair coloring and founds L'Oreal

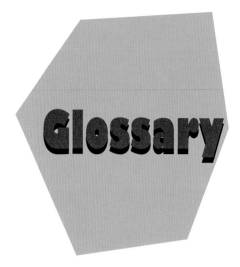

Glossary

binder: a substance that causes a pigment to adhere to a surface

blatta: a purplish red dye made from the mucus of certain sea snails

calico: a cotton fabric painted or printed with designs in two or more bright, fast colors

chromophore: a chemical that absorbs light of certain wavelengths

cochineal: a tiny round parasitic insect that lives on the opuntia cactus and contains carminic acid; a red dye

color subtraction: a process by which objects that do not emit light absorb and reflect light waves so that they are perceived as colored

direct dye: a dye that is bonded to a textile with ionic bonds

fast: permanent

henna: a plant-based dye used to redden hair

indigo: a blue dye made from indigo plants

indigofera: the active coloring element of indigo

indirect dye: a dye that requires a mordant to bind it to a textile

kermes: an insect containing kermesic acid that lives on oak trees near the Mediterranean Sea and in Asia Minor; a red dye made from kermes

madder: a plant whose roots, when dried and ground, were used as a red dye; a red dye

mordant: a chemical that reacts with both a dye and a textile or leather and binds them together

pigment: a microscopic piece of a colored material that is suspended (not dissolved) in a liquid and applied to the surface of an object to color it

saffron: a spice and dye made from the stigmas of the *Crocus sativus* plant

sumptuary laws: laws enforced in the Middle Ages and Renaissance that regulated dress and personal habits, and were designed to limit what legislators viewed as extravagant behavior

synthetic dye: a man-made dye

vat dye: a dye, such as indigo, that is insoluble in water but can be broken down by chemical processes and inserted into the structure of a textile fiber

woad: a plant containing indigofera found in northern Europe whose leaves produce a deep blue dye

For More Information

BOOKS

Adrosko, Rita. *Natural Dyes and Home Dyeing*. New York: Dover Publications, 1976.

Dean, Jenny. *The Craft of Natural Dyeing*. Kent, England: Search Press Ltd., 1995.

Delamare, Francois, and Bernard Guineau. *Colors: The Story of Dyes and Pigments*. New York: Harry N. Abrams, 2000.

Epp, Dianne. *The Chemistry of Natural Dyes*. Middletown, OH: Terrific Science Press, 1995.

Van Stralen, Trudy. *Indigo, Madder, and Marigold*. Loveland, CO: Interweave Press, 1993.

WEB SITES

members.aol.com/PinteaReed/books.html
> For books about dyes and dyeing

www.parentsplace.com/schoolage/fun/gen/0,8728,11957,00.html
> For recipes for natural dyes

weaving.about.com/library/weekly/aa062100.htm
> For recipes for natural dye

Index